# TROMBONE
# 101 JAZZ SONGS

Available for
FLUTE, CLARINET, ALTO SAX, TENOR SAX, TRUMPET,
HORN, TROMBONE, VIOLIN, VIOLA, CELLO

ISBN 978-1-4950-2343-9

**HAL•LEONARD®**
**CORPORATION**
7777 W. BLUEMOUND RD. P.O. BOX 13819 MILWAUKEE, WI 53213

Visit Hal Leonard Online at
**www.halleonard.com**

# CONTENTS

# ALL OF ME

TROMBONE

Words and Music by SEYMOUR SIMONS
and GERALD MARKS

# ALL THE THINGS YOU ARE

TROMBONE

Lyrics by OSCAR HAMMERSTEIN II
Music by JEROME KERN

# APRIL IN PARIS

TROMBONE

Words by E.Y. "YIP" HARBURG
Music by VERNON DUKE

# AUTUMN IN NEW YORK

TROMBONE

Words and Music by
VERNON DUKE

# AUTUMN LEAVES

TROMBONE

English Lyric by JOHNNY MERCER
French Lyric by JACQUES PREVERT
Music by JOSEPH KOSMA

# BEWITCHED

Words by LORENZ HART
Music by RICHARD RODGERS

TROMBONE

# BEYOND THE SEA

Lyrics by JACK LAWRENCE
Music by CHARLES TRENET and ALBERT LASRY
Original French Lyric to "La Mer" by CHARLES TRENET

TROMBONE

# THE BLUE ROOM

TROMBONE

Words by LORENZ HART
Music by RICHARD RODGERS

# BLUE SKIES

TROMBONE

Words and Music by
IRVING BERLIN

# BLUESETTE

TROMBONE

Words by NORMAN GIMBEL
Music by JEAN THIELEMANS

# BODY AND SOUL

TROMBONE

Words by EDWARD HEYMAN,
ROBERT SOUR and FRANK EYTON
Music by JOHN GREEN

# BUT BEAUTIFUL

TROMBONE

Words by JOHNNY BURKE
Music by JIMMY VAN HEUSEN

# CAN'T HELP LOVIN' DAT MAN

TROMBONE

Lyrics by OSCAR HAMMERSTEIN II
Music by JEROME KERN

**Moderately and rather freely, with a lilt**

# CARAVAN

TROMBONE

Words and Music by DUKE ELLINGTON,
IRVING MILLS and JUAN TIZOL

# CHARADE

TROMBONE

By HENRY MANCINI

# CHEEK TO CHEEK

TROMBONE

Words and Music by
IRVING BERLIN

# COME RAIN OR COME SHINE

TROMBONE

Words by JOHNNY MERCER
Music by HAROLD ARLEN

# Dancing on the Ceiling

TROMBONE

Words by LORENZ HART
Music by RICHARD RODGERS

# DEARLY BELOVED

TROMBONE

Music by JEROME KERN
Words by JOHNNY MERCER

**Moderately**

# DO NOTHIN' TILL YOU HEAR FROM ME

TROMBONE

Words and Music by DUKE ELLINGTON
and BOB RUSSELL

# DON'T GET AROUND MUCH ANYMORE

TROMBONE

Words and Music by DUKE ELLINGTON
and BOB RUSSELL

# DREAMSVILLE

TROMBONE

By Henry Mancini

# FALLING IN LOVE WITH LOVE

TROMBONE

Words by LORENZ HART
Music by RICHARD RODGERS

# A FINE ROMANCE

TROMBONE

Words by DOROTHY FIELDS
Music by JEROME KERN

# FLY ME TO THE MOON
### (In Other Words)

TROMBONE

Words and Music by
BART HOWARD

# GEORGIA ON MY MIND

TROMBONE

Words by STUART GORRELL
Music by HOAGY CARMICHAEL

# HERE'S THAT RAINY DAY

TROMBONE

Words by JOHNNY BURKE
Music by JIMMY VAN HEUSEN

# HERE'S TO LIFE

TROMBONE

Music by ARTIE BUTLER
Lyrics by PHYLLIS MOLINARY

# HONEYSUCKLE ROSE

TROMBONE

Words by ANDY RAZAF
Music by THOMAS "FATS" WALLER

# HOW DEEP IS THE OCEAN

(How High Is the Sky)

TROMBONE

Words and Music by
IRVING BERLIN

# HOW INSENSITIVE
### (Insensatez)

Music by ANTONIO CARLOS JOBIM
Original Words by VINICIUS DE MORAES
English Words by NORMAN GIMBEL

TROMBONE

# I CAN'T GET STARTED

TROMBONE

Words by IRA GERSHWIN
Music by VERNON DUKE

# I COULD WRITE A BOOK

TROMBONE

Words by LORENZ HART
Music by RICHARD RODGERS

# I GOT IT BAD AND THAT AIN'T GOOD

TROMBONE

Words by PAUL FRANCIS WEBSTER
Music by DUKE ELLINGTON

# I'LL REMEMBER APRIL

TROMBONE

Words and Music by PAT JOHNSTON,
DON RAYE AND GENE DE PAUL

# I'M BEGINNING TO SEE THE LIGHT

TROMBONE

Words and Music by DON GEORGE, JOHNNY HODGES,
DUKE ELLINGTON and HARRY JAMES

# I'VE GOT THE WORLD ON A STRING

TROMBONE

Words by TED KOEHLER
Music by HAROLD ARLEN

# IF I WERE A BELL

TROMBONE

By FRANK LOESSER

# IMAGINATION

TROMBONE

Words by JOHNNY BURKE
Music by JIMMY VAN HEUSEN

# IN A SENTIMEMTAL MOOD

TROMBONE

By DUKE ELLINGTON

# IN THE WEE SMALL HOURS OF THE MORNING

TROMBONE

Words by BOB HILLIARD
Music by DAVID MANN

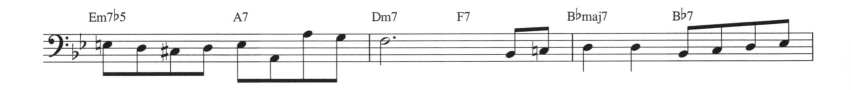

# INDIANA
## (Back Home Again in Indiana)

TROMBONE

Words by BALLARD MacDONALD
Music by JAMES F. HANLEY

**Moderately, with a lilt**

# ISN'T IT ROMANTIC?

TROMBONE

Words by LORENZ HART
Music by RICHARD RODGERS

# IT COULD HAPPEN TO YOU

Words by JOHNNY BURKE
Music by JAMES VAN HEUSEN

TROMBONE

**Moderately**

# IT DON'T MEAN A THING
### (If It Ain't Got That Swing)

TROMBONE

Words and Music by DUKE ELLINGTON
and IRVING MILLS

# IT MIGHT AS WELL BE SPRING

TROMBONE

Lyrics by OSCAR HAMMERSTEIN II
Music by RICHARD RODGERS

# THE LADY IS A TRAMP

TROMBONE

Words by LORENZ HART
Music by RICHARD RODGERS

# LAZY RIVER

TROMBONE

Words and Music by HOAGY CARMICHAEL
and SIDNEY ARODIN

**Moderate Swing**

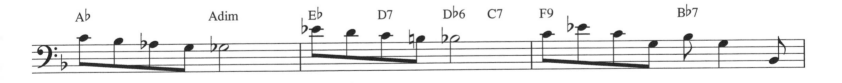

# LET THERE BE LOVE

TROMBONE

Lyric by IAN GRANT
Music by LIONEL RAND

# LIKE SOMEONE IN LOVE

TROMBONE

Words by JOHNNY BURKE
Music by JIMMY VAN HEUSEN

# LITTLE GIRL BLUE

TROMBONE

Words by LORENZ HART
Music by RICHARD RODGERS

# LONG AGO (AND FAR AWAY)

TROMBONE

Words by IRA GERSHWIN
Music by JEROME KERN

# LOVER, COME BACK TO ME

TROMBONE

Lyrics by OSCAR HAMMERSTEIN II
Music by SIGMUND ROMBERG

# LULLABY OF BIRDLAND

TROMBONE

Words by GEORGE DAVID WEISS
Music by GEORGE SHEARING

# LULLABY OF THE LEAVES

TROMBONE

Words by JOE YOUNG
Music by BERNICE PETKERE

# MANHATTAN

TROMBONE

Words by LORENZ HART
Music by RICHARD RODGERS

# MEDITATION
## (Meditação)

TROMBONE

Music by ANTONIO CARLOS JOBIM
Original Words by NEWTON MENDONÇA
English Words by NORMAN GIMBEL

# MIDNIGHT SUN

Words and Music by LIONEL HAMPTON,
SONNY BURKE and JOHNNY MERCER

TROMBONE

# MISTY

TROMBONE

Music by ERROLL GARNER

**Slowly, with a smooth Swing**

# MOOD INDIGO

TROMBONE

Words and Music by DUKE ELLINGTON,
IRVING MILLS and ALBANY BIGARD

# MOONLIGHT IN VERMONT

TROMBONE

Words by JOHN BLACKBURN
Music by KARL SUESSDORF

# More Than You Know

Words by WILLIAM ROSE and EDWARD ELISCU
Music by VINCENT YOUMANS

TROMBONE

# MY HEART STOOD STILL

TROMBONE

Words by LORENZ HART
Music by RICHARD RODGERS

# MY OLD FLAME

TROMBONE

Words and Music by ARTHUR JOHNSTON
and SAM COSLOW

# MY ONE AND ONLY LOVE

TROMBONE

Words by ROBERT MELLIN
Music by GUY WOOD

# MY ROMANCE

TROMBONE

Words by LORENZ HART
Music by RICHARD RODGERS

# MY SHIP

TROMBONE

Words by IRA GERSHWIN
Music by KURT WEILL

# THE NEARNESS OF YOU

TROMBONE

Words by NED WASHINGTON
Music by HOAGY CARMICHAEL

# A NIGHT IN TUNISIA

TROMBONE

By JOHN "DIZZY" GILLESPIE
and FRANK PAPARELLI

# ON GREEN DOLPHIN STREET

TROMBONE

Lyrics by NED WASHINGTON
Music by BRONISLAU KAPER

# ONE NOTE SAMBA
## (Samba de uma nota so)

TROMBONE

Original Lyrics by NEWTON MENDONÇA
English Lyrics by ANTONIO CARLOS JOBIM
Music by ANTONIO CARLOS JOBIM

# PICK YOURSELF UP

TROMBONE

Words by DOROTHY FIELDS
Music by JEROME KERN

# POLKA DOTS AND MOONBEAMS

TROMBONE

Words by JOHNNY BURKE
Music by JIMMY VAN HEUSEN

# QUIET NIGHTS OF QUIET STARS
## (Corcovado)

TROMBONE

English Words by GENE LEES
Original Words and Music by ANTONIO CARLOS JOBIM

# SATIN DOLL

TROMBONE

By DUKE ELLINGTON

# SKYLARK

TROMBONE

Words by JOHNNY MERCER
Music by HOAGY CARMICHAEL

# SO NICE
## (Summer Samba)

TROMBONE

Original Words and Music by MARCOS VALLE
and PAULO SERGIO VALLE
English Words by NORMAN GIMBEL

# SOPHISTICATED LADY

TROMBONE

Words and Music by DUKE ELLINGTON,
IRVING MILLS and MITCHELL PARISH

# SPEAK LOW

TROMBONE

Words by OGDEN NASH
Music by KURT WEILL

# STELLA BY STARLIGHT

TROMBONE

Words by NED WASHINGTON
Music by VICTOR YOUNG

# STOMPIN' AT THE SAVOY

TROMBONE

By BENNY GOODMAN,
EDGAR SAMPSON and CHICK WEBB

# STORMY WEATHER
## (Keeps Rainin' All the Time)

TROMBONE

Lyric by TED KOEHLER
Music by HAROLD ARLEN

# A SUNDAY KIND OF LOVE

TROMBONE

Words and Music by LOUIS PRIMA, ANITA NYE LEONARD,
STANLEY RHODES and BARBARA BELLE

# TANGERINE

Words by JOHNNY MERCER
Music by VICTOR SCHERTZINGER

TROMBONE

**Easy Swing**

# THERE'S A SMALL HOTEL

TROMBONE

Words by LORENZ HART
Music by RICHARD RODGERS

# THESE FOOLISH THINGS (REMIND ME OF YOU)

TROMBONE

Words by HOLT MARVELL
Music by JACK STRACHEY

# THE THINGS WE DID LAST SUMMER

TROMBONE

Words by SAMMY CAHN
Music by JULE STYNE

**Moderate Swing**

# This Can't Be Love

TROMBONE

Words by LORENZ HART
Music by RICHARD RODGERS

# THOU SWELL

TROMBONE

Words by LORENZ HART
Music by RICHARD RODGERS

# UNFORGETTABLE

TROMBONE

Words and Music by
IRVING GORDON

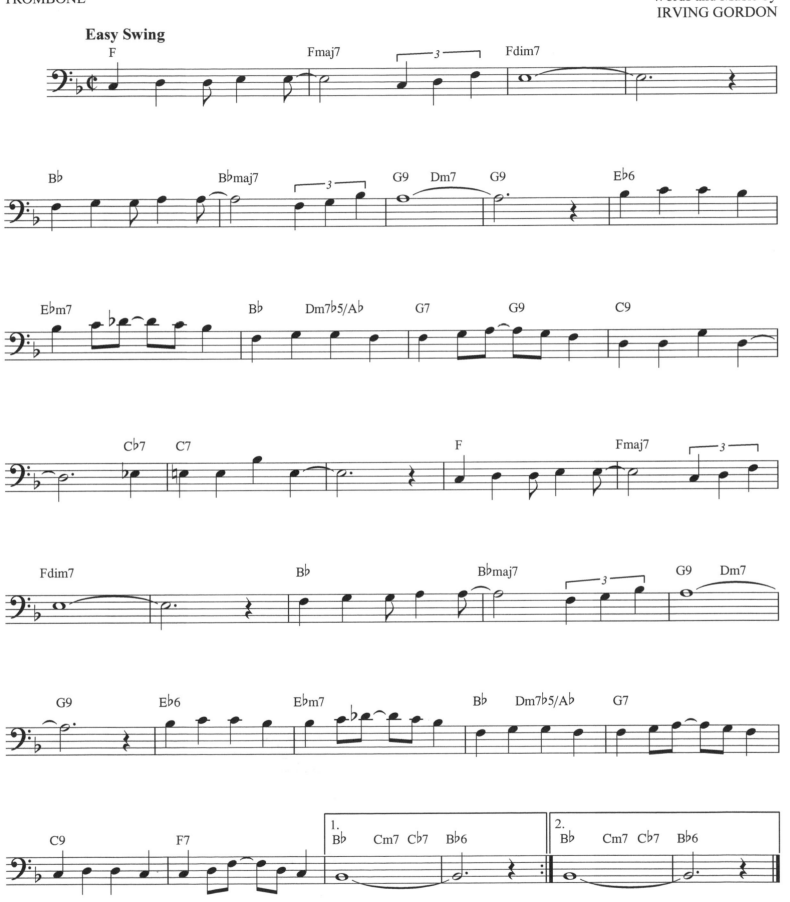

# THE VERY THOUGHT OF YOU

TROMBONE

Words and Music by
RAY NOBLE

**With a slow, easy Swing**

# WATCH WHAT HAPPENS

Music by MICHEL LEGRAND
Original French Text by JACQUES DEMY
English Lyrics by NORMAN GIMBEL

TROMBONE

# WAVE

TROMBONE

Words and Music by<br>ANTONIO CARLOS JOBIM

# THE WAY YOU LOOK TONIGHT

TROMBONE

Words by DOROTHY FIELDS
Music by JEROME KERN

# WHAT'LL I DO

TROMBONE

Words and Music by
IRVING BERLIN

# WILLOW WEEP FOR ME

TROMBONE

Words and Music by
ANN RONELL

# WITCHCRAFT

TROMBONE

Music by CY COLEMAN
Lyrics by CAROLYN LEIGH

# YESTERDAYS

TROMBONE

Words by OTTO HARBACH
Music by JEROME KERN

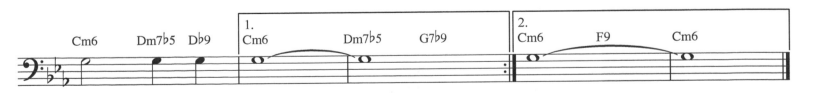

# YOU ARE TOO BEAUTIFUL

TROMBONE

Words by LORENZ HART
Music by RICHARD RODGERS

# YOU BROUGHT A NEW KIND OF LOVE TO ME

TROMBONE

Words and Music by SAMMY FAIN,
IRVING KAHAL and PIERRE NORMAN

**Medium Swing**

# YOU DON'T KNOW WHAT LOVE IS

TROMBONE

Words and Music by DON RAYE
and GENE DePAUL